101 Animal Jokes for Kids

This is a work of fiction. Names, characters, places, and incidents either are the product of the author's imagination or are used fictitiously. Any resemblance to actual persons, living or dead, events, or locales is entirely coincidental.

www.themkids.com

QUESTION

Where do cows go for entertainment?

ANSWER

The mooo-views!

QUESTION

What do you call a sleeping bull?

ANSWER

A bull-dozer!

QUESTION

What did the farmer call the cow that had no milk?

ANSWER

An udder failure.

QUESTION

What do you call a bear with no ear?

ANSWER

B!

QUESTION

What did the farmer call the cow that had no milk?

ANSWER

An udder failure.

QUESTION

QUESTION

What do you get when you cross a snake and a pie?

ANSWER

ANSWER

Pie-thon!

QUESTION

What animals are on legal documents?

ANSWER

Seals.

Why didn't the boy
believe the tiger?

He thought it
was a lion!

QUESTION

What fish only swims at night?

ANSWER

A starfish.

QUESTION

Why is a fish easy to weigh?

ANSWER

**Because it has
its own scales!**

QUESTION

Why did the turkey cross the road?

ANSWER

To show everyone he wasn't chicken!

QUESTION

**Why do fish live
in salt water?**

ANSWER

**Because pepper
makes them sneeze!**

QUESTION

Where do polar bears vote?

ANSWER

The North Poll.

Why did the pony have to gargle?

Because it was a little horse!

QUESTION

What time does a duck wake up?

ANSWER

At the quack

QUESTION

**Why are fish
so smart?**

ANSWER

**Because they
live in schools.**

QUESTION

What happened when the lion ate the comedian?

ANSWER

He felt funny.

What time is it when an
elephant sits on the fence?

Time to fix
the fence!

QUESTION

What did the dog say when he sat on sandpaper?

ANSWER

RUFF!

QUESTION

What is a cat's favorite color?

ANSWER

Purrr-ple.

QUESTION

**What do you
give a sick bird?**

ANSWER

Tweetment.

What kind of bird works at a construction site?

The crane.

QUESTION

Why are cats good
at video games?

ANSWER

Because they have
nine lives!

QUESTION

**What do you call
a sleeping dinosaur?**

ANSWER

A dino-snore!

QUESTION

What song does a cat like best?

ANSWER

Three Blind Mice.

QUESTION

**What do you call
a funny chicken?**

ANSWER

A comedi-hen!

QUESTION

**Why did the snake
cross the road?**

ANSWER

**To get to the
other sssssside.**

Why are dogs
like phones?

Because they
have collar IDs.

QUESTION

**What came after
the dinosaur?**

ANSWER

It's tail!

QUESTION

What is a rabbit's favorite dance style?

ANSWER

Hip-hop!

QUESTION

What do you call a cow that won't give milk?

ANSWER

A milk dud!

QUESTION

**What did the
sick chicken say?**

ANSWER

**Oh no!
I have the people-pox!**

QUESTION

What type of markets do dogs avoid?

ANSWER

Flea markets!

QUESTION

What did the dinosaur use to build his house?

ANSWER

A dino-saw.

QUESTION

Why do seagulls like
to live by the sea?

ANSWER

Because if they lived by the
bay they would be bagels!

What was the
elephant's favorite sport?

Squash.

QUESTION

Have you ever
seen a catfish?

ANSWER

How did he hold
the rod and reel?

QUESTION

Why did the lion
spit out the clown?

ANSWER

Because he
tasted funny.

QUESTION

When does a teacher carry birdseed?

ANSWER

When there is a parrot-teacher conference!

What time is it when ten elephants are chasing you?

Ten after one!

QUESTION

How can you tell which
rabbits are getting old?

ANSWER

Look for the
grey hares.

How can you best raise a
baby dinosaur?

With a crane!

What do you call a group of rabbits hopping backwards?

A receding
hare line.

QUESTION

Why do gorillas
have big nostrils?

ANSWER

Because they have
big fingers.

QUESTION

How do bees
get to school?

ANSWER

By school buzz!

Why do gorillas
have big nostrils?

Because they have
big fingers.

What do you call a
fish without an eye?

Fsh.

QUESTION

**What do you call
a bruise on a T-Rex?**

ANSWER

A dino-sore!

Why did the cat
go to Minnesota?

To get a mini soda.

QUESTION

Where do orcas hear music?

ANSWER

Orca-stras!

QUESTION

Why did the cow
cross the road?

ANSWER

To get to
the udder side.

QUESTION

Why do pandas like old movies?

ANSWER

Because they are black and white.

What do you do if your dog
chews a dictionary?

Take the word
out of his mouth!

QUESTION

What is a
pirate's favorite's fish?

ANSWER

A swordfish!

QUESTION

What is a frog's favorite year?

ANSWER

Leap year!

QUESTION

What is a cat's favorite breakfast?

ANSWER

Mice krispies.

QUESTION

Where do
horses live?

ANSWER

In the
neigh-borhood.

QUESTION

What did the porcupine say to the cactus?

ANSWER

Is that you mommy?

QUESTION

What is a lion's favorite state?

ANSWER

Maine.

QUESTION

What do you call a cow that twitches?

ANSWER

Beef jerky.

**What do you call
a messy hippo?**

A hippopota-mess!

QUESTION

What do camels use to hide themselves?

ANSWER

Camelflauge!

What's black and white and red all over?

A sunburnt zebra.

QUESTION

What's a puppy's favorite kind of pizza?

ANSWER

Pupperoni.

QUESTION

Who makes dinosaur clothes?

ANSWER

A dino-sewer.

QUESTION

What do you call a dinosaur that never gives up?

ANSWER

**A try and try
and try-ceratops!**

QUESTION

What did the dog say to the flea?

ANSWER

Stop bugging me!

QUESTION

What do you call a deer that costs a dollar?

ANSWER

A buck.

QUESTION

Why did the dinosaur cross the road?

ANSWER

The chicken wasn't around yet.

QUESTION

What do you call snake with no clothes on?

ANSWER

Snaked.

QUESTION

What's an alligator's favorite drink?

ANSWER

Gator-ade.

What kind of mouse does not eat, drink, or even walk?

A computer mouse.

QUESTION

What do you call a dog with a Rolex?

ANSWER

A watch dog.

QUESTION

What kind of mouse does not eat, drink, or even walk?

ANSWER

A computer mouse.

QUESTION

What do you give
a pig with a rash?

ANSWER

Oinkment.

QUESTION

What's a dog's favorite food for breakfast?

ANSWER

Pooched eggs.

What do you call a dog that
likes bubble baths?

A shampoodle!

QUESTION

What kind of dog always runs a fever?

ANSWER

A hot dog.

**Why did the policeman give
the sheep a ticket?**

**He made an
illegal ewe turn.**

QUESTION

Where are sharks from?

ANSWER

Finland.

**What do you call
a mad elephant?**

An earthquake.

QUESTION

What is a shark's favorite sandwich?

ANSWER

Peanut butter and jellyfish.

QUESTION

What do you call a mommy cow that just had a calf?

ANSWER

Decalfinated!

QUESTION

**What is a
cow's favorite place?**

ANSWER

The mooseum.

QUESTION

What do fish take
to stay healthy?

ANSWER

Vitamin sea.

QUESTION

Why did the policeman give the sheep a ticket?

ANSWER

He was a baaaaaad driver.

How do you keep a skunk
from smelling?

Plug it's nose.

QUESTION

What did the Cinderella fish wear to the ball?

ANSWER

Glass flippers.

QUESTION

Why was the mouse
afraid of the water?

ANSWER

Catfish.

QUESTION

What do you get from a bad-tempered shark?

ANSWER

As far away as possible.

QUESTION

Why did the elephant
leave the circus?

ANSWER

He was tired of
working for peanuts.

QUESTION

What do you call a gorilla wearing earmuffs?

ANSWER

Anything you like, he can't hear you.

QUESTION

Why are giraffes so
slow to apologize?

ANSWER

It takes them a long time
to swallow their pride.

QUESTION

What's the difference between a fish and a piano?

ANSWER

You can't tuna fish.

QUESTION

What did the banana do
when the monkey chased it?

ANSWER

The banana split!

QUESTION

What kind of cat should you never play games with?

ANSWER

A cheetah!

QUESTION

What do you call a dinosaur in a car accident?

ANSWER

A tyrannosauraus wreck!

QUESTION

**How do you
catch a squirrel?**

ANSWER

**Climb up a tree and
act like a nut!**

QUESTION

Where do fish keep
their money?

ANSWER

In a river bank!

QUESTION

What would happen if pigs could fly?

ANSWER

The price of bacon would go up.

QUESTION

How do you stop an
elephant from charging?

ANSWER

Take away
his credit card!

THE END!
WE HOPE
THESE MADE
YOU SMILE!

Made in the USA
Middletown, DE
29 November 2019